Discover America

Spoiled for Choice

The United States is so large and there's so much to see, you could take a hundred vacations, without ever once leaving the country, and still not see it all.

So how do you find out about the places you are most likely to enjoy going to see?

One of the best ways is by talking to your friends and finding out from them where they've been and what they enjoyed seeing and doing. But remember, a vacation is for all the family, so be prepared to compromise.

Another good place for information is your local library or bookstore. And if that's not enough, then the Internet is a vast storehouse of information— sometimes, however, the sheer volume of information means that it's difficult to find the real nuggets.

Here are just a few destination ideas for you to think about.

Williamsburg, Virginia
As well as Colonial Williamsburg, the first permanent English colony in America is also nearby —Jamestown. Don't miss the local museum and find out about the real Pocahontas. You will also be able to see replicas of the ships that brought the early settlers to America.

Disney World and Universal Studios, Florida
Orlando must be one of the most popular vacation destinations in the entire country, featuring the twin attractions of Universal Studios and Disney World. If you feel like a change of scenery while you are there, then Cocoa Beach is nearby, as is the Kennedy Space Center.

Mount Rushmore, South Dakota

The idea behind the project to create the enormous carved heads of George Washington, Thomas Jefferson, Theodore Roosevelt, and Abraham Lincoln was to attract extra tourists to the region. The task took Gutzon Borglum and his 400 workers from 1927 until 1941 to complete. Each head is 60 feet high.

National Civil Rights Museum, Tennessee

Memphis, Tennessee is home to the National Civil Rights Museum. Here you will see the most famous bus in America—the one on which Rosa Parks was arrested back in 1955 for demanding her civil rights. Learn about all the major events in the Civil Rights movement.

Monterey Bay Aquarium, California

This world-famous aquarium studies and exhibits many different species of marine creatures. You might be interested in trying the Habitats Path Tour while you're visiting.

Washington, D. C.

The national capital could be renamed "museum heaven." Try the National Air & Space Museum for a start and then see how you like the National Insect Collection at the Museum of Natural History. You can also visit the National Zoo and feel close to history at the Washington Monument or Lincoln Memorial.

Wrigley Field, Illinois

This is thought by many people to be one of the most beautiful ballparks in the country, and it is home to the Chicago Cubs baseball team. It was built almost 100 years ago, in 1914, and it is the third oldest ballpark in the major leagues. Buy some tickets and see a ballgame.

Yellowstone National Park, Wyoming

Parts of this national park are also found in Montana and Idaho. The park covers an area of about 3,500 square miles and is famous for its bears, moose, and other wildlife, but also for its hot springs, boiling mud, and "Old Faithful," a geyser that can shoot 8,000 gallons of boiling water nealy 200 feet into the air.

New York — A World City

In 1626 the Dutch bought the 13-mile-long island of Manhattan from a group of Native Americans. Dutch settlers named it New Amsterdam. Later, the Dutch surrendered the island to the British, who renamed it New York.

In 1898 the surrounding areas of Queens, Brooklyn, Staten Island, and the Bronx joined Manhattan to form New York City. By 1900, thousands of immigrants from all over the world were arriving daily to swell the numbers of people living in what was already the largest city in the country. Tall buildings were put up to accommodate the city's workers. In 1902 the first of the many skyscrapers that would form Manhattan's famous skyline was completed. It was called the Flatiron Building.

Over the years, thousands of African-Americans moved from the southern states and settled in New York City. Many lived in Harlem, in northern Manhattan, which became a center of African-American literature, art, dance, and music.

Today, New York is a magnet for visitors from other parts of America and from all over the world. It has some of the world's best known art galleries, as well as being home to the many theaters found on glamorous Broadway. And on Wall Street, the famous stock exchanges buy and sell many billions of dollars of stocks and shares each year.

N.Y.C. TAXI

7B72

New York's top ten

The ten sites attracting the most tourists each year in New York City are:

Empire State Building

Fifth Avenue

Rockefeller Center

Statue of Liberty

Ellis Island Immigration Museum

Times Square and Broadway

Central Park

Metropolitan Museum of Art

"For hire" light

American Museum of Natural History

Chinatown

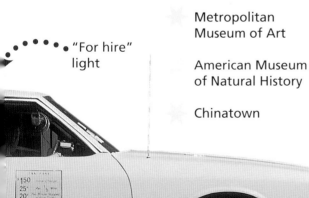

Yellow cab

Ask people what comes to mind when thinking about New York, and most will mention the city's famous yellow taxis.

Plan a Trip

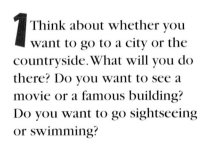

What would you do if you had to plan a trip? How would you decide where to go? How would you get there? And what would you do once you arrived? It's good to have a plan before you start!

Plan your destination

The first thing to do is choose where to go on your trip.

You will need

- Travel magazines
- Globe or atlas
- Computer connected to the internet
- Local street map
- 2 rulers
- Paper and pencil
- String

1 Think about whether you want to go to a city or the countryside. What will you do there? Do you want to see a movie or a famous building? Do you want to go sightseeing or swimming?

2 Ask friends and neighbors. Visit the library for ideas. Read leaflets and magazines about trips you could take. Look at a map or globe.

3 Learn more about the place you want to visit. Ask an adult to help you find out information about this place on the Internet.

Use a map

Using a street map will help you to plan a short trip to a place of interest once you have decided on the general place to visit.

1 Open the map and find the list of street names.

2 Find your street on the list. There will be a code made up of a letter and a number.

3 Look along the edge of the map where you will see letters on one edge and numbers on another. Find the letter and the number of your street.

4 Lay one ruler along the line with the letter in your code. Take the other ruler and lay it across the number in your code. Your street is in the square where the two lines meet.

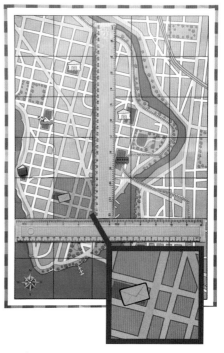

Plan a route

A map will help you plan a route for your trip.

1 Look at the symbols in the map's key to help you find a place to visit, such as a museum or park.

2 Use the grid lines on the map to find that place. Draw a circle around it.

3 Draw a line along the streets that connect your starting point to the place you want to visit.

4 Place a piece of string along the route. Mark the string at both ends.

5 Find the map scale to find the distance you will have to travel.

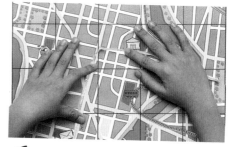

6 Use the ruler and the map scale to find the answer.

BEWARE OF
SNAKES!
PLEASE STAY
ON DESIGNATED
TRAIL

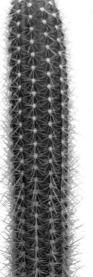

Games and Puzzles

Where in the country?

See how many locations of the following monuments, buildings, or tourist destinations you can identify. You need to give the state and/or city, depending on how they are usually identified.

1 Chrysler Building

2 Bryce Canyon

3 Waimea Bay

4 Kennedy Space Center

5 Fisherman's Wharf

6 Harvard University

7 Madison Square Garden

8 Yosemite National Park

9 Comiskey Park

10 Grand Ole Opry

11 Golden Gate Bridge

12 Laguna Beach

13 Arlington National Cemetery

14 Everglades

Scrambled letters

See if you can find the word hidden in these scrambled letters.

Did you know?

We all know the expression "as American as apple pie," but in the 19th century when apples were in short supply, there was a recipe for mock apple pie, which was made from sugar, spices and CRACKERS!

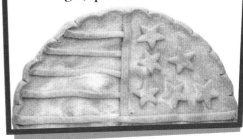

State flags
Can you identify the state flags pictured here?

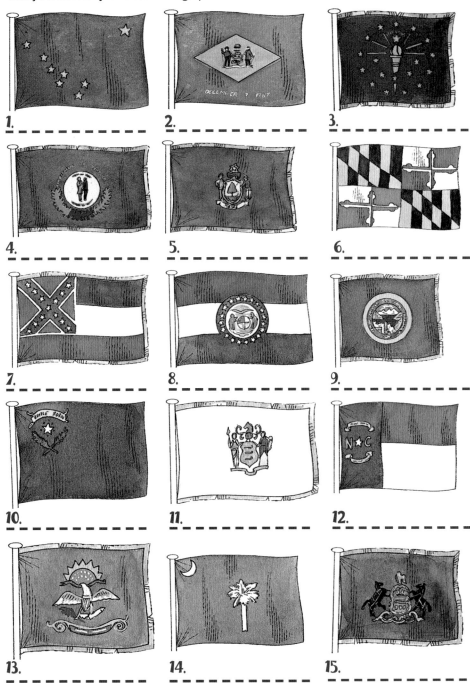

1.

2.

3.

4.

5.

6.

7.

8.

9.

10.

11.

12.

13.

14.

15.

For answers to all puzzles, see page 16.

The Grand Canyon

Arizona's awe-inspiring Grand Canyon National Park has 2 billion years of the Earth's history carved in its rock. The park covers an area of almost 2,000 square miles and attracts more than 5 million visitors each year.

There were three main objectives when the Grand Canyon National Park was first set up in 1919. First, it was to protect the native people living in the region. Second, it was to protect local wildlife. And third, it was to protect and preserve the landscape itself.

At more than a mile from the rim to the floor, the Grand Canyon is one of the world's deepest canyons. At its widest point, the canyon is an amazing 18 miles across, while its total length is 275 miles.

When the sunlight strikes the cliffs at the right angle you can easily see the different layers of rock that make up the canyon walls—layers that have built up over 2 billion years. At the bottom of the canyon, the rock is so old that it existed long before the dinosaurs lived on the Earth.

The Grand Canyon's top ten

The ten features attracting most attention from visitors to the national park are:

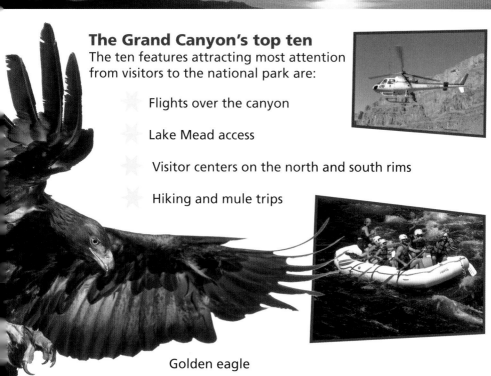

- Flights over the canyon
- Lake Mead access
- Visitor centers on the north and south rims
- Hiking and mule trips

Golden eagle

Wildlife

The Grand Canyon has several habitats and many of the animals living in them are rare or endangered. Near the river, coyotes, skunks, tree frogs, and rattlesnakes are found. Above the inner canyon, bats and California condors can be seen. While forested areas have lizards, owls, porcupines, squirrels, black bears, gray foxes, and elk.

- Yaki, Grandview, and Moran lookout points
- Whitewater rafting
- Kaibab squirrels
- Tusayan Village
- Golden Eagles
- Purple lupines

Getting down

There are hiking trails leading down to the bottom of the canyon, but many visitors prefer to ride mules down instead.

Gray fox

Did you know?

The two words most used by visitors to describe the Grand Canyon are "overwhelming" and "humbling."

Christopher Columbus

Born in 1451 in the Republic of Genoa, which is now part of modern-day Italy, Christopher Columbus would eventually become famous for discovering something he was not even looking for!

In about 1470, at the age of 19, Columbus found himself shipwrecked. He came ashore in Portugal (a country on the west coast of Spain), where he would later return, marry, and have a child. Sadly, his wife died soon after childbirth and Columbus moved to Spain with his infant son.

The adventurer in Columbus was fascinated by sailors' stories of new lands waiting to be discovered in the Atlantic Ocean. He'd read all he could about geography and studied all the available maps and charts. You need to know that at this time in history whole continents were yet to be discovered by Europeans. And even with the countries they knew existed, there was still much doubt about where exactly they were. Maps had large blank areas indicating "the unknown," and often there would be a warning note to sailors that read: "Here be dragons."

Columbus formulated an ingenious plan. Using the best information available at the time, he became convinced that he could open up a new and quicker trade route to the East (specifically India) by sailing in a westerly direction. By this time, it was generally accepted that the world was indeed round rather than flat.

In order to get the money and the ships he needed to put his plan into action, Columbus initially asked the king of Portugal to help him. But he refused. Next, he tried the king and queen of Spain. After hearing him out, they, too, said no. But he tried again and again to interest them and eventually they agreed to finance his expedition.

You might already know the rhyme used to remember the year Columbus set out on his voyage of discovery: "In 1492 Columbus sailed the ocean blue." In fact, it was August 3 of that year that Columbus's three ships—*Nina*, *Pinta*, and *Santa Maria*—set sail from Palos in Spain.

Long after Columbus had expected to find land there was still nothing on the horizon. Despairing and on the point of turning back, defeated and empty-handed, there came the call he'd been praying to hear from the lookout high in the ship's rigging. "Land Ho!" It was now October 12, and they had been at sea for more than two months.

Although Columbus was convinced the land he had discovered was an island somewhere in Asia, in reality it was probably San Salvador. Although wrong about where he was, he managed to transport back to Spain enough gold to ensure that the king and queen would willingly support his next adventure.

In total, Columbus made four voyages to the "New World," landing on many Caribbean islands before discovering the South American mainland. He never did find North America, however, and he died at home in Spain in 1506 still firmly believing that the lands he'd been exploring all those years were part of Asia.

Photo Tips

The best way to remember all the places you have visited is by starting a collection of photographs. Here are some tips to help you get the best from your camera.

Use the viewfinder or screen to make sure you don't cut off important parts of the subject—such as a person's head.

Keep dirty fingers well away from the camera lens.

Move in close when photographing people. Either move physically closer or zoom in with the lens.

Keep the camera level so that pictures don't run uphill or downhill.

Take some of your pictures (especially of tall subjects such as buildings) with the camera on its side.

The main subject sometimes looks better if it is off to one side and not right in the middle of the picture.

Find a shooting position that includes objects in the foreground if it is looking too empty.

Follow a moving subject, such as a running figure or car, with the camera as you take the picture. This will cause the background to blur while the subject remains sharp.

Always have spare film or a fresh memory card, and always have spare batteries to fit your camera.

Answers to puzzles on pages 10–11

Where in the country? 1 New York City; **2** Utah; **3** O'ahu, Hawaii; **4** Florida; **5** San Francisco, California; **6** Boston, Massachusetts; **7** New York City; **8** California; **9** Chicago, Illinois; **10** Nashville, Tennessee; **11** San Francisco, California; **12** California; **13** Virginia; **14** Florida; **15** Washington, D.C.

State flags: 1 Alaska; **2** Delaware; **3** Indiana; **4** Kentucky; **5** Maine; **6** Maryland; **7** Mississippi; **8** Missouri; **9** Nebraska; **10** Nevada; **11** New Jersey; **12** North Carolina; **13** North Dakota; **14** South Carolina; **15** Pennsylvania.

Scrambled letters: Tourism.

A TRICK HALLOWEEN

BY ANNA KOPP

For my boys, whose love of Minecraft
fuels their love of reading.

It's Halloween night, and best friends Gump and Chosie are going trick-or-treating.

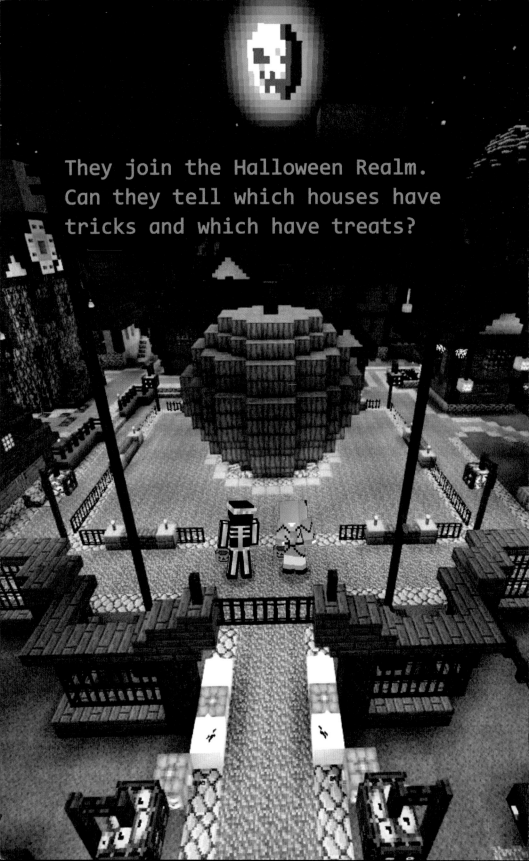

They join the Halloween Realm.
Can they tell which houses have
tricks and which have treats?

The first house looks bright and inviting. It even has a sign.

The third house has creepy
spiders and sticky webs.

EEK!

The fifth house
is very green.
How strange.

Gump and Chosie go to Halloween Park.

They ride the roller coaster.

WHEEEE!

They got the best treat after all.

Made in the USA
Middletown, DE
20 September 2021